156 QUESTIONS
ABOUT

HOW TO PREVENT RECESSION

156 QUESTIONS

ABOUT

HOW TO PREVENT RECESSION

USING ANCIENT WISDOM
&
MANAGEMENT IDEAS

SATYA SAURABH KHOSLA

AFTER PREDICTING THE 2008 RECESSION, AUTHOR SHOWS A WAY TO PREVENT ONE

PARTRIDGE
A Penguin Random House Company

To order additional copies of this book, contact
Toll Free 800 101 2657 (Singapore)
Toll Free 1 800 81 7340 (Malaysia)
orders.singapore@partridgepublishing.com

www.partridgepublishing.com/singapore

?

Is it possible to prevent a recession?
It is possible to predict a recession and also to prevent
it. *'How to Prevent Recession – using ancient wisdom
and management ideas'* shows how to do both.
For prediction an individual's skill is sufficient.
However, prevention needs collective effort. So, this
book gives a theory that binds, in a common string,
all pearls of inspiring actions that help society today.

**Why is the prediction of the 2008 recession
given at the back of the main book?**
What is the point of predicting if you cannot change
things for the better? The effort to prevent a recession
is more important for society. So, the contents of how to
prevent it precede the prediction. For those interested,
the prediction is given in the beginning of this booklet.

How to get a recap of 'How to Prevent Recession'?
The common threads that can bind society are the four
goals of life for man or the 4Cs. They prevent recession
and a *Summary* of this is given at the end of this booklet

"The author seeks that word 'Man' be read as gender neutral in this book. Man can be a pun on the Hindi word 'Mun' where 'a' - if sounded as 'u' – means mind of a human being. The idea of education is to train the mind - for life. Therefore, ideas here are about 'Man Management'. 'Managing' the mind helps man and firm to prevent social problems. Common goals and strategy for man and firm creates unity in action at home, work – for the benefit of society. Ancient techniques can help direct thoughts of man, plans of firm. Just as four Purusharthas give meaning to man's actions – making them fit for society, 4C's give meaning to a firm.": Extract from Preface of book 'How to Prevent Recession - using Ancient Wisdom and Management Ideas'

2008:
All managers thought they were successful.

Their companies earned record profit, they received record bonus.

Yet society discovered later that their actions led to the recession.

The failure of such success never hurt society harder.

> *The Prediction about Goldilocks growth:*
> *"__When in late '07 the interest rates are__*
> *__adjusted upwards, severe pain is likely to be__*
> *__felt__ (an estimated $ 1 trillion on ARMs i.e.*
> *adjustable rate mortgage, will be reset)."*

Ancient wisdom: Why a story of Goldilocks?
Since time immemorial stories have been used to explain difficult ideas. Jesus used parables. A financial parable explains an idea - which was unbelievable in late 2007.

Management Idea:
"The best way to predict your future is to create it": Peter Drucker. How to create a future without recession? This is the primary task addressed.

"The 2008 recession came at a time when nobody thought anything could go wrong. Some were tempted to think that 'there is no harm if I buy assets a little more than what I can afford – will only help the economy grow – after all asset prices are increasing'. All those who thought like this may or may not have caused the recession – but some of them were affected by it.

Economists gave this growth a name – 'Goldilocks' growth. This is a story we have heard as children. Goldilocks got all she wanted despite the danger of losing her way and entering a bear's house. She ate their porridge, broke a chair, slept but left as a friend of the bear family. The growth economists talk of was like the porridge she ate – neither too hot nor too cold. It was just right. Goldilocks growth, too, is not too hot to cause inflation nor too cold to cause recession. Everybody gets what they want. With low unemployment, low interest rates allow taking loans and almost everybody's income grows - along with stock markets and asset prices. It seemed like that in the first decade of the new millennium ...till something went wrong as 2008 approached.": Excerpt from the book.

Ψ

PREDICTION OF ECONOMIC RECESSION PUBLISHED ON OCTOBER 4, 2007*

The USA equity markets started falling around 14th to 16th October 2007. It was thought to be a healthy correction, at that time...till it cascaded. In 2008 this movement downwards of the stock markets was recognised as a recession.

Contents of the article:
<u>The Story of Goldilocks in the house of 'Bears'</u>

Will cheap credit and hedges make her lead the world markets into the house of 'Bears'?

Goldilocks has strayed away from home once again. Deep in the forest of the global economy, Goldilocks has found a "safe" resting place – Where porridge and lodging is free. Just like credit (well, almost – in Yen carry trades). The 3 bears of "twin deficits", liability of retiring "baby boomers" and "excess liquidity, cheap credit" turn out to be friends after all.

Like Papa Bears porridge, some issues (like twin deficits) are too hot to handle and, therefore, irrelevant. Some others, like Mama Bears porridge (fate of retiring "baby boomers"), leave Goldilocks stone cold and, therefore, can be ignored. What Goldilocks loves is the porridge of Baby Bear full of cheap credit & uncontrolled spending. This she can lap up till she falls asleep (sadly, after breaking the very chair on which she eats).

The three bears do not return Goldilocks favour of gobbling up the porridge by doing the same to her. Instead, they call out to a fleeing Goldilocks and invite her to keep supping with them whenever she likes. Goldilocks has been doing so for some time now.

This "true" story of global growth is referred to as a "Goldilocks" situation by economists today.

The Story of US housing

Goldilocks prefers the borrowed house of bears to sleep and eat her porridge. Sleeping in a borrowed house is dangerous when the bears mood changes.

From 2001-2005 outstanding mortgage debt in US had risen 68% to 8888 billion $: an unparalleled debt expansion. Borrowing to own a house is easy when interest rates are low and "easy" cash is chasing borrowers. Repaying the same loan when interest rates are high may imply a liability much larger than what the buyer can afford. This is more so if the loan was a little beyond the means of the buyer to begin with and / or his subsequent income stream does not increase to match the new liabilities. When rates increase from 5% to 7% that implies: a 40% increase in amount of interest to be paid. US Fed fund rates have risen from 1% to 5.25% in last few years.

Why should a loan be given to a buyer who can barely afford it? There are reasons. Firstly, if the lending bank can push the risk of default (by selling these loans) to Fannie Mae (ultimately, US taxpayers) or to buyers of Mortgage backed securities then the risk of default is not on the banks books – Even though it remains in the system. Secondly, the extreme competition among lenders to capture the same "prime" target audience of homebuyers forces them to expand to "sub prime" borrowers who have dubious or no credit record.

Consequently, home prices in the US today are not in any known relationship with either rents or salaries. Many homeowners complain that rents are less than half of mortgage payments. Salaries, for many, cover only short-run repayment using adjustable interest rates. When in late '07 the interest rates are adjusted upwards, severe pain is likely to be felt (an estimated $ 1 trillion on ARMs i.e. adjustable rate mortgage, will be reset). According to a typical "exploding" ARM sub-prime loan, buyers are considered qualified for loan if the original ("teaser") monthly payment is not higher than 61% of their post-tax income. The scheme works out such that in 2 years, without interest rate increase, the repayments become 96% of purchaser's income.

Goldilocks lost in "Hedges"

The Goldilocks economy has witnessed an explosive growth in derivatives. The housing loans, in a low credit risk environment, like many other transactions, were converted into derivatives. The size of these derivative transactions, used to "hedge" risks of Goldilocks growth, is many times larger than the jungle of global growth itself. Financial innovation has replaced technological innovation as the support system to global growth today.

The outstanding volume of derivative transactions is growing annually at 54%, while global nominal GDP is growing at less an 8% in dollar terms. If this rate of growth continues till end '08 the total outstanding derivates would cross 1,000,000 billion USD. Some estimate that the total volume of derivatives is over 60 times global M1, more than 12 times M2 and about 8 times global GDP.

In Goldilocks world every $ of GDP is being hedged 8 times or every demand deposit 60 times. Most of these hedges are done at historically low volatilities. Crisis occurs at high volatilities. We have seen what volatility in Mid-August did to equity prices the world over. Surprisingly 90% of these derivate transactions are on the books of a dozen global banks.

Nobody knows the collective impact of these derivative transactions in a financial crisis. Just as nobody knows what will happen to Goldilocks when the bears mood changes. The last time this impact was tested in 1998, outstanding derivatives were less than quarter of the current volume. The New York Fed had to undertake a dramatic rescue, supported by the same major banks that hold almost all the derivative paper today.

Of course, the objective behind most of the hedging transactions would have been to mitigate unnecessary risk or seek return. However, where the growth of derivatives is so much larger than the growth of global GDP, there is a high probability of some derivative transactions that are not funded by adequate capital. These pose a risk to the global financial system in a period where consistent & continuous volatility upsurge happens.

While liquidity has generated asset bubbles, the risk of these bubbles has been "hedged" with derivatives and financial innovation. When will a pinprick burst a bubble? This is always difficult to forecast.

Financial innovation sometimes presents weakness as strength. Initially, excessive global liquidity allows the less credit-worthy to borrow more than they earlier could and now should. The big banks add fuel to the fire of credit expansion when they don't hold this debt but sell it to others through securitization. Sadly, each bank believes that risk 'removal' is taking place by distributing debts 'far & wide so that no single holder has significant exposure'. In reality, risk has spread for while derivatives do insure 'a holder against losses', but the sale of this risk to many small buyers spreads it in a manner that almost everybody will now be impacted.

"It is only a story...."

It is true that Goldilocks is a story meant only for children. Also, using parables was relevant only during the time of Jesus. While the risk of Goldilocks growth being unable to extricate itself from the "hedges" threatens to become real, one question inevitably arises: "Will the porridge of "cheap credit" and the shade of 'Hedges' make Goldilocks lead the world markets into the house of 'Bears'?"

*Contents of the above article were published in Business Times, Singapore on October 4, 2007. Please refer front page title 'A Financial Parable' and editorial page.

What can we learn from the failure of success in 2008?

"Success is a goal of life for many. But, success depends on many factors. Many of them are outside the control of man. Sometimes success, earning wealth and fame etc. does not satisfy man. In some cases it leads to greed.

When greed is not restrained it leads to many social problems, including recession. Managers felt they were succeeding in 2008, too – yet society experienced a recession.

Excellence is also possible through man's conscious effort, reforming habits, control of mind and refining of character. The desire of excellence, too, is never ending. The only difference is that it seeks to bring out the best 'within' man, for himself and society, without greed.

This is called Self Actualisation in management/ psychology and is a goal of life in ancient Indian tradition. Awareness about it was created as the basis of action in life – which includes man's actions in firm.

Creating awareness of the potential of excellence 'within' man was the task of education in ancient India. It helped overcome greed and, thus, prevented recession. This book details how this awareness is created and used to impart skills of management that lead to balance 'within' man and society. Such a 'balance' prevents recession."

Excerpt from the Synopsis of the book: 'How to Prevent Recession - using Ancient Wisdom and Management Ideas'

1

WHAT WAS THE MOST IMPORTANT CAUSE OF THE RECESSION?

Ancient wisdom:
Theory of Karma states that previous actions could have caused current events. Explore to find a cure...

Management Idea:
"Every action has an opposite and equal reaction"

A law of physics that can be used by management to explore the cause that led to the reaction (Recession).

- *A diagnosis is successful if it leads to prevention of the disease in future. A successful diagnosis identifies conditions that will enable prevention in future*
- *A change in habits is usually necessary for effective prevention. A change in habits emerges if there is a change in ideas of man.*
- *A new Awareness leads to new ideas that enable prevention. Prevention is better than cure.*

Translating ancient remedies for preventing recession:

Four simple translations of words used in ancient Indian texts - in modern management language. These, and other such concepts or ideas, help integrate ancient wisdom with management thought for application in life:

Moksha = man achieves his potential for excellence, Maslow's Self Actualisation: Self Satisfaction leads to it.

God = Goodness + simultaneous Excellence in all dimensions (Man in search of God in ancient India is same as management theory of In Search for Excellence)

Nishkama Karma = Selfless Love in action; refer Geeta.

Self Preservation, Self Sacrifice, Self Satisfaction, Self Realistion = equivalent ideas of wisdom used in book for Maslow's need hierarchy stages as man transforms Swartha (selfishness) to Parartha (higher good) to Parmartha (highest good of all) through Purushartha...

What was the most important cause of the recession?
It was the failure of many ideas that man believed in.

How is it possible to prevent recession?
Reform of ideas is the first step. It leads
to reform of man and society.

How is this reform possible?
It begins with reform of man when his actions emerge
from ancient wisdom. We will give some examples here.

Which idea can educate man to enable such reform?
When the interconnectedness of man, society and nature
becomes clear many social problems including recession
disappear. Academic theory should help make man see it
clearly. In the experience of ancient Indians the practice
with discipline of achieving four goals of life or 4Cs or
Purusharthas enabled this Truth to emerge from within
man over time. The 4C Approach seeks to adapt this
approach to the study of management theory for best
practices in life and at work - changing ideas of success.

**Change in idea of success: Success that
harms others and society leads to failure**

**What can replace success as the goal of man's
effort? Why choose wisdom to guide man?**
Some ideas are needed when success also fails. If ideas
of success could not prevent the recession, maybe
some wise old ideas can, if made relevant to today's
circumstances. Ancient wisdom must use today's idiom.

What does Wisdom lead to? It leads to success based on values and character: This is excellence
A sincerity about achieving excellence
leads to self actualisation.
Though it is the larger goal, other goals help
achieve it –both in life and at work.

The book talks of the idea of Awareness as Part A. What is Awareness?
Realising the real value of human values is awareness. It is also realising the interdependence of man and society.

How does it help man in daily life?
If value of something is realised, it is worthwhile to use it. When values are used in life and at work there is balance within man leading to balance in society.

But, how does that prevent recession?
A recession refers to an act of reduction or moving back, not forward. Preventing a recession would imply effectively blocking movement backward. When humans recede from their natural state, they recede into selfishness. Then, instead of helping each other they indirectly or directly cause harm
The impact on society of the summation of
such individual actions is recession.
For, it is in basic human nature to care for
others. Values prevent recession of man into
selfishness and society into a recession.

This statement nobody doubts, but how does it work?
It all starts with Unity of thought word and deed of
man. When such co-operation within man with ethics
leads to sincere co-operation with all – the foundation is
ready. It only needs a focus on whatever task is executed
with a concern for society. The output, then, expresses
individuality while changing competitive response too.

**Recession can be prevented by changing
ideas about competitive behaviour**

$$\underline{\leq} \div$$

*(Many ideas deal with dividing $\div$ society into groups
that benefit while others may be harmed. Discharge of
polluting effluents in rivers is an example that benefits
a few people for short time only while causing long
term irreversible damage of inestimable cost. The sum
of benefits to society may sometimes be less than $\leq$ the
benefit to a group of individuals. Such selfishness, when
expressed in other myopic actions, leads to a recession)*

Many current ideas esp. those about competitiveness need
to be changed for this.

Present ideas of competitiveness are based on the assumption
of comparing achievements of one's company, industry,
society, nation with others. This can lead to jealousy which
signifies the end of consciousness of man about his potential.

In fact the expression of competitiveness, if expressed
through selfishness, can become the core of the problem.
It reflects the inadequacy of ideas that benefit society.

**But, how does wisdom change ideas of
competitiveness and prevent recession?**
Comparing with others is the very initial stage of
competitiveness. When man, companies, industries
discover their potential of adding value to society
by expressing their individuality – they serve the
customer in their own unique way. Sometimes, all
are copying each other in some way or the other.
This experience of one's individuality comes only
through a deeper sensitivity about self, customer and
society. When such individuality is experienced, the
only competition is with one's own past work. Society
has yet to fully experience such creativity – which
comes naturally after practice of ancient wisdom.
Today we face problems of over exploitation of
resources and harmful waste material –for many try
to do the same thing using the same resources or
they just pump up demand by unnecessary product
obsolescence leading to wastage of resources and
material that harms the environment. We have only
reached the level of thinking of recognising that above
activities cause harm. How can this be stopped needs
a very different approach which can be inculcated
by proper education which promotes excellence.

**So can we say this book is a value based
guide to living life and doing work?**
That is one possible description.

Why include management theory in such a guide?
Education is always practical. If academics
can be integrated with daily life and work in
discipline of management study, it is possible to
integrate the same with all other disciplines.

**How can wisdom of religions help
man in a search for excellence?**
All religions have three aspects:

1. A common message of: adhere to Truth, follow
   morality with Love and Peace.
2. Differences in philosophy, beliefs: about existence
   of a creator and His nature.
3. Cultural aspects of religions: customs differ and
   can even change with time.

This book uses the first aspect and interprets the second
to benefit man and society.

How can these ideas be spread through education?
Education imparts skills and specialisation. If the impact
of their use on society is not visualised, it is like seven
blind men trying to cure an elephant using their vision.

How are education and spirituality connected?
Transformation of ideas through education leads to
transformation of skills. When actions are done in
the right spirit, this is spirituality. Both education and
spirituality create balance within man and society.

How is this different from the current approach?
Current ideas concentrate on economic reforms. These reforms operate in the context of society. So, society should be reformed, first. Society consists of humans, so reforming ideas and convictions of man is needed.

What is the role of secular education?
Secular education and education based on values (spiritual education) are like two wings of the same bird. If a bird tries to fly on one wing it is likely to crash. The problems of crime, social conflict, and recession emerge due to a lack of conviction in following values. This conviction can best be inculcated in the schooling years.

Will a recession come again?
"I'm sure a crash like 1929 will happen again. The only thing is that one doesn't know when. All it takes for another collapse is for the memories of the last insanity to dull." *John Kenneth Galbraith.*

What makes prediction of a recession possible?
It is possible by observing facts from point of view of society. Visualising totality of impact of actions is a key.

How do we learn which facts are more relevant?
When interconnectedness of man and society is clear, Truth emerges from 'within'. Discrimination helps decide which facts are more relevant. Discrimination gives the ability to 'C' or see Truth behind distortions.

How to develop the ability to see 'C' the Truth?
The book is only a catalyst for helping this.

So you admit reading it cannot prevent recession?
Reading any book cannot prevent it. Absorbing its ideas
and implementing it in daily life will always help.

Why involve *Purusharthas* in life and management?
Every activity has a goal. Simple activities like going to
a supermarket or school also have a purpose to fulfill.
Then how can 60 or 70 years of life have no purpose?
So, righteous conduct, economic activity, fulfillment of
desires and action detached from results are goals of life.

How are goals of life used for companies or firms?
The book is about life and managing it – both at home
and work. Both paths lead to balance in society. Diagram
6.0 shows this. Purposeless activity cannot create
balance within man – or in society. Different words or
explanations are used to describe these goals for firms.

Why do you keep using the words strategy of life?
Any activity performed to achieve a goal through
some method is strategy. So, activities performed to
achieve goals of life should be called strategy of life!

Why confuse strategy used by companies with life?
Strategy – or a way of achieving a goal – should be
same at work and home. Both should be based on truth
and morality. Then there will be no conflict within man
or in society. Righteous conduct is the first goal of life.

***Purusharthas* is being imported into education. Can you give an idea we know and merge it with wisdom?**
Purusharthas is not being imported. Human activity should be goal directed for it to be fruitful. Business calls it strategy. The idea is the same. Another similar idea is Self Actualisation, the highest order need of man as given by Maslow. We can compare it to *Moksha*.

But *Moksha* is a goal of life...Maslow never said so...
Is it not in the fitness of things to make the highest order need of man the highest goal he seeks to achieve? *Moksha* is to be lived and achieved – through action. This book recaps the way shown by ancient wisdom.

What is importance of the article predicting the 2008 recession?
The article was published days before USA equity markets started a fall cascading to the 2008 recession. Readers should know how to prevent a recession.

How to develop the ability to predict a recession?
The book seeks to develop society's ability to do so. This process can only start with each individual – when readers become thought and action leaders in society.

2

WHAT IS THE BOOK ABOUT?

Ancient Wisdom:
*"Education is not for **living** but for **life**"*

Management Idea:
*"There is nothing more powerful than an idea whose time has come" The time has come for man to educate himself in ideas that create balance, prevent recession. Then, out-come of actions determines nature of in-come he seeks. Ideas that give excellence in **Life** guide him. For, even animals follow instinct, enabling act of **Living**.*

Ideas that integrate (mathematical symbol : ∫) man with society prepare man for what can be called the business of living life. Then life moves forward for both (▶) through balance within man that enables balance in society. Education ideas create the base of such balance.

If man lived alone he would only use his basic instincts for survival and protection from forces of nature.

Society allows him to take advantage of the skills of others and contribute his own for others benefit. Business involves give and take. Living in society involves living life by giving of one's talents to benefit others and taking from them the products of their skills.

Of all ideas the book of life is written with, the most important is the idea of business of living life. For the same balance that is created in man (through education ideas) is used for creating balance in society.

Recognising this interdependence, why can we not have a common strategy for business and life that ensures such balance?

What is the subject matter of the book?
It is about how to manage living life in society.

Why does it sound like a business management book?
Business involves give and take. When man lives in society he indulges in give and take of both emotions and money. Normally, emotions, too, need to be reciprocated for them to endure. Society promotes this.

So why use management ideas for emotions also?
The theory of how to live life should be simple. It is based on managing the human mind. The idea of interdependence is basic for society. All subjects of study should come out of a simple theory. Otherwise, conflict between living life and its practice can result.

If each individual lives life from a different angle, why choose the management angle?
Well, all of us use management ideas to manage life, time, work... Also, recession is blamed on business. If life can use ideas of business strategy to prevent recession, then can we blame business theory for it?

If faulty business strategy led to the recession why study ideas of business strategy?
This has already been answered. Not all ideas of strategy are faulty. It is their use by the human mind which leads to problems. The mind needs to be trained.

That does not answer another question –
why should we study strategy?

Strategy is a way of achieving a goal – any goal. So, the contexts of using its ideas can be many. If strategy is used for achieving the goal of life, it is Strategy of Life. If used for business, it is a business strategy.

If strategy can be used for wrong goals why use it?

A knife with a surgeon benefits while if given to a murderer it can harm. Using a tool incorrectly is the fault of the human mind. The same ideas of strategy can be integrated with the noblest spiritual ideas used to serve the noblest goals that wisdom sets for man.

Life should be based on Love. Why call it business?

Selfless Love is noble and helps elevate life. It should apply to business also – to make society prosper. Ideas of business thinkers, too, can be elevated to enrich life.

We know that we are living to do business.
What is this business of living life?

Life is about how you keep it busy – with good deeds or otherwise. This busy-ness of life is its business. If deeds help others and society the giving to society and taking from it is mutually supportive and, therefore, it is successful busy-ness. Give and take should not become a zero sum game i.e. what you take from society is not a loss to society. A non zero sum game is that in which the gain of one party does not become the loss of the other.

Please do not indulge in fantasies. We work to gain – someone will have to lose for us to gain...No?
Does the tree lose something if you pluck its ripe fruit? In fact it continues to grow and prosper and give more fruit. If society benefits from your effort, it does not diminish you. In fact, it only gives an opportunity to increase your skill further, an opportunity to understand more and perform better the next time. Each rendering of service is an opportunity to improve skills. When such a humble attitude is ingrained, there is no question of loss. The same logic applies to the person serving you in society. Education should instill such motivation. Then there is no loss – only gain for both parties.

Have you forgotten the role of money here?
The primacy of money is in the mind of man. What man needs is a service or a product not money. He has no use of the physical form otherwise. Will you care for a bank note if it is demonetised? It is human effort that is the real currency to be exchanged. If this is directed towards excellence, the value of the nation's moral currency can increase by its own without fluctuating easily.

Again you have not answered the question – do we not work to earn money?
Yes, we work to earn money – but for its capacity to buy things. Excellence increases the capacity to buy by increasing the capacity to give. This is the mutual interdependence among members of society. Education must make man experience this interdependence for the business of life to be fruitful.

Does this not sound like a moral education class?
When you go to the market place you expect everybody
to follow morals. Are you not angered or hurt by
cheating? The same holds true when others use your
service or product. If all give the best, all get only the
best. This is excellence at work in a non zero sum way.

**But we have courses in ethics – what
more do you expect now?**
Theory gets life not from classes on ethics but by best
practices. The focus is on the word practice. It is practice
of theory that gives life to theory and society. That was
the purpose of education and management education.

Again it is not clear – what are you saying?
It is not the courses that are important. If what is taught
is not being put into practice then either the technique
is wrong or the assimilation is not there or the whole set
of steps of teaching and learning needs to be revisited.

So... what are you suggesting?
Teach a practice that adds value to life. Then, it will
add value to the business of life. Then it will add value
to business. This will enable excellence and balance.

Are you trying to say that we are not doing this?
Of course everybody is trying to do this only.
The question is how far we are successful.

How can you make such an accusation?
Asking such questions does not reflect spirit of learning.

Now, does that sound like an even bigger accusation?
No. If you get good marks in only one subject but fail
the sum total of all subjects even the school hesitates
to give you a degree. Today if society suffers despite
decisions made by educated people, the question is: have
we cleared the sum total of all subjects put together?

Is this not academic blasphemy?
Surprisingly not... True educators love honesty
and healthy criticism. All of them love their
profession. It saddens them that the same student
who topped has gone and made a mess of society.
They were bound to give high marks for he
knew how to beat the system. Sadly the habit of
beating the system did beat the system. It led to
a recession. So, can we have a new system?

What can education institutions do?
Sadly, by the time a child reaches 18 years of age many
habits are formed. The best time to inculcate values is
earlier. However, many practices are given in the book.
If a student follows any one practice like speaking the
truth softly and sweetly other things will follow. The
educational institution can enable this through learning
curriculum that incorporates such ideas and practices.

3

WHY SHOULD I READ THIS BOOK?

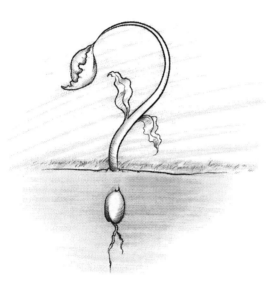

Ancient wisdom:
The seed of wisdom sprouts by asking the right question
?The gap between two thoughts is wisdom?

Management Idea:
"The most serious mistakes are not being made as a
result of wrong answers. The true dangerous thing
is asking the wrong question." Peter Drucker

The habit of asking questions leads to progress – for man and society.

Ancient wisdom asks a question that is often ignored:

"Can mans ability to think emerge from matter?"

If not, then why so much effort to study matter alone?

The body follows the dictates of that which is invisible: the human mind. A study of the technique to control and direct the mind gives purpose to life. Purpose gives life to each activity.

The most important question for business is to define the

purpose of business. Finding the purpose before performing any activity leads to goal oriented behavior.

Any activity directed to fulfilling a goal is called strategy. The idea of strategy emerges from the ability of asking the right question.

Why should I read this book?
Questions about purpose should be posed.
The habit of asking why leads to ancient
wisdom. If questions are asked with pure
intention the reader is ready for wisdom.

How does this question lead to wisdom?
Sooner or later these questions expand, leading to 'why
was I born?' – Which leads to 'what is the purpose
of life?' Ancient wisdom is about the experiences
gained while searching for purpose of life.

What is gained from ancient wisdom?
Ancient wisdom leads to transformation of man.

What is the benefit of transformation?
Transformation makes man satisfied. It gives
permanent happiness or bliss. It also enables
harmony in society. Harmony within man and
in society prevents recession, conflict, crime
and sensitises about harmony with nature.

India is not so prosperous, why choose its tradition?
The idea is to learn from ancient civilisations. Was there
something in their ideas that helped society sustain?
The effort is to use such ideas in today's social context.

Why study its ideas of wisdom for prosperity?
If a civilisation has survived some prosperity can be assumed. However, two facts help our choice. Firstly, there were many attacks and conquests faced here. If there was no prosperity, there is no need for such attacks or desire to conquer it. Secondly, there is no record of attack on other nations by this civilisation. This shows that either they were committed to peace or were self satisfied with their own material progress – or both.

If society is not giving my salary why bother about its transformation?
All of us depend on air for living. Similarly many resources are common and shared. If they are misused by one person it will not be noticed. But if all think like this, it harms everybody.

If after transforming you want me to make less money, then I am not interested...
Money cannot give happiness though it can give many things to make life comfortable. It is not about earning less or more. It is about earning in a manner that gives happiness too.

OK, then what should be the basis of my earning?
Learning should be the basis of earning – learning how to live life. Living is a continuous activity, so is learning.

**Now don't confuse the issue – where does
learning and life come into this?**

Earning is used to live life. Learning makes living life
useful. If life is not useful for others, society is harmed.

**Can you say it in simple words – what should
I learn so that I can earn and be happy?**

The importance of society is the first thing to
be learnt. If you harm others while earning, it is
like harming yourself. So, never hurt others or
society as you earn. This gives happiness to all.

**Man's actions, should be guided by *Bhava Adwaitha*
not *Karma Adwaitha*. Can you explain...?**

Man should feel that he is that there is no difference
between him and others. This removes the feeling of
false satisfaction he gets by hurting others or stealing
from them. For, then, it is like hurting yourself or
stealing from one self. This is *Bhava Adwaitha.*

**This is understood. Why should this
feeling not be implemented?**

That is a wrong interpretation.

What is the correct interpretation?

Though there should be no differences felt in
attitude towards others, yet in the real world there
are physical differences. These cannot be ignored.
Actions must be within the constraints of physical
differences that exist in the world. This is the practical
application of knowledge that leads to wisdom.

Can you give an example of its practical application?
The book gives the example of having equal feeling in the heart for the king and the farmer. Yet, in practice, the king's status has to be given due worldly respect.

What is the benefit of *Bhava Adwaitha*?
Bhava Adwaitha ensures purity of intention towards others and society. Just as the intention in using a knife by a doctor is different from the intention of a murderer. Society benefits only when intentions are pure. *Bhava Adwaitha* performs this most important role.

4

I LIKE PROFIT! CAN WE HAVE A PROFITABLE CONVERSATION?

Current mind management ideas:
When there is a bull in the stock markets, investors are overjoyed. When there is a bear they are depressed.

Ancient Wisdom for training the mind:
It is profitable in life not to be overjoyed by success or depressed by failure. Righteous conduct trains the mind.

Some things that make the business of life profitable: Success fails when profit becomes the only prophet i.e. it is treated as something whose pursuit is more important than core values that bind society: Truth, Righteous conduct, Peace and Selfless Love.

Seeking excellence in all actions gives joy. It is a natural expression of the inner joy within. This natural joy is seen in the natural smile of each child. Excellence is never forced; it comes from the Source within us.

The desire for excellence overarches both success and failure. This attitude of being detached – but doing the right thing just because it is to be done – is true profit.

When the mind is trained to do what is the right thing to do – without fear of failure or greed for success – excellence results with ease.

Success is a hand maiden of excellence!... *Sooner or later, it follows meekly...so long as you do not look over the shoulder to see if it is coming. This success lasts...*

You talk a lot about profit. What is the nature of profit that led to the recession?

There is a time when innovation that serves others is the pride of society. Then this innovation is used for selfish or destructive ends like bombs. This begins the decline.

What led to the recession?

Greed. How? There can be many explanations. Some prefer the explanation that when innovation became too much of hard work, ideas of financial innovation came.

What did it result in?

It gave profits without commensurate increases in productivity. Using leverage beyond limits is greed.

But leverage also has risks...

Sadly, these risks were passed on to unsuspecting people. Success in earning such profit was the hallmark of smartness. This smartness led to adverse consequences for all.

How was profit maximised?

Maximising leverage led to maximising profit. This also maximised the risk. Humpty Dumpty!

Is all financial innovation bad? Taking debt, too, can be considered as such...

Part B of the book is titled: Study of Limits. Everything within limits can be useful. Intentions are most important. The purity of intention increases through a search for excellence.

What makes success different from excellence?
If you succeed in achieving excellence, there is no
difference. False ideas about success led to the recession.
The idea of success is enlarged by using excellence.

**If I maximise my profit, which *Dharma*
(righteous conduct) prevents me?**
Each one of us has a right to act so
long as it does not hurt others.

**So, how can my maximising profit
harm others or society?**
Each act is in a different context. If maximising
becomes a habit then discrimination can be lost. Habits
lead to repetitive behavior. Each situation can be unique
and may require a unique response. If rules are followed
blindly, computers not humans can run the world.

What is discrimination – can you give an example?
Let us say a cab driver sees someone dying on the road -
should he save a life by taking him to the hospital or
wait to assess whether he will be paid for this service?

**But, if he does not charge money – will
others not misuse this kindheartedness?**
That risk is there but discrimination that led him
to protect the patient may protect the driver.
This is the inner meaning of:
Dharmo rakshati rakshatah

**So, discrimination is not indiscriminate
action but involves full use of intelligence?**
Not just intelligence but its application to all
information – starting from purity of enquiry.

**What if the cab driver gets a hefty reward
from the family, if the patient survives?**
If the very thought of reward enters his head,
the act becomes impure. Next time he will use
intelligence to assess if the person being helped
is capable of surviving and rewarding.

What is the harm with such an assessment?
The nature of such assessment is against
the nature of business itself.

Why and how?
Ancient Wisdom states that the purpose of
business is to do yeoman service to society.

**Is not transporting people or
helping them such a service?**
Of course it is. The eye, while doing service, should not
be on profit but on best services. Profit will be a natural
hand maiden of such an effort. It will meekly follow.

**Who is there to judge the difference between
selfish and selfless service? Nobody will know...**
...except the conscience of man. It bestows Self
Satisfaction – that leads to the purpose of life.

What if I get more satisfaction from earning money?
Of course earning money is important but not the sole
purpose of business. The satisfaction of saving a life or
contributing in a significant way to others is a moment
treasured forever. It will slowly give skills and insights.

Should I accept a reward for saving the life?
Accepting or not accepting a reward is a personal
decision. It is taken according to circumstances
and the inner nature of the receiver.

**What circumstances can impact a
decision to accept reward?**
If accepting it is necessary, then accepting it is OK. If
social norms dictate it or it is being used as an example
for others, one can accept. Its use depends on you.

What is the most important thing about the reward?
The most important thing is that there
should be no expectation of reward.

If that is taken seriously we will never make a profit.
This is only a fear. If reward (profit) is in the
mind, nobody will help those in need. If helping
others is at the top of the mind, the nature of
help melts human hearts and bonds society.

Does that mean we indulge in charity all the time?
The thought should be of giving service. Profit
is a by-product of the effort undertaken.

That does not answer the question

For one act of helping so many questions arise.
No one asks a question when profit is made.

The idea of business is not clear without profit

Without profit no business survives. The business
of life is not based on profit. Serving society
makes the business of life profitable. Fair profit is
automatically understood when idea is to serve.

What is fair?

Society expects man to seek excellence. This shifts
ideas away from selfishness. When work becomes
worship, greed slowly goes away. Ideas of what is fair,
then, emerge from the experience of self satisfaction.

Is that not subjective?

Man has a freedom to decide. Emergence of excellence
and removal of selfishness takes time. Excellence leads
to self confidence and self satisfaction. Lack of greed
emerges only after basic needs of self preservation are
met and a feeling of self satisfaction is experienced
through working selflessly and serving society.

What does excellence seek?

Excellence seeks the joy of expressing individuality
and delivering value in a unique way. When satisfaction
emerges, the natural desire is to be fair to all. The idea
of fair profit comes naturally. Self confidence leads to it.

Is Self confidence not the anti thesis of humility?

Self confidence is not arrogance of 'I Know better'.
Humility emerges from recognising the ever changing
nature of things. Self confidence arises from knowing
this fact with humility – it motivates us to keep learning.

Does humility not imply a lack of confidence?

Such humility never leads to excellence. Humility is
based on knowing that knowledge is ever expanding.
It is to be upgraded. To serve, we have to identify
with needs of others by observing, seeking, listening.
Understanding such requirement fully gives confidence.

How does this confidence relate to my business?

The ability to understand that each customer is unique
makes it possible to fulfill his needs in a unique way.
Understanding and continuously upgrading knowledge
to satisfy this uniqueness – uniquely – gives confidence.

But, profit is like breathing for man – without
it will business not die, despite confidence?

Of course... Ancient Indian tradition talks about control
of breath for a healthy and happy life. Some believe that
slowing this breath leads to a longer, self confident and
healthy life. So answers are many, understanding is One.

Is this the reason why profit is mentioned in
Part B of the book in 'Study of Limits'?

Yes.

**What should be the motive of earning profit
and what should be its expression?**
Non attachment should be the motive and
service to society the expression.

How does this non attachment work?
Take the example of a cab driver. Non attachment makes
him help those in need without any expectation. Service
is the natural expression of business and its true profit.

But I thought it was non attachment to taking reward
That is the same thing – emerging
from the same motive.

**If non attachment is the motive then
what should be the purpose?**
These are words. The purpose is to always seek
excellence. This gives purpose to life and business.
Words should not detract from this purpose or motive.

**If non attachment is the motive, how
can we be attached to excellence?**
The silence of wise seems to concede defeat when words
are used to prove smartness. The spirit of learning is in
humility. Spiritual ideas capture the spirit of living life.

That does not answer the question
Words are inadequate to capture the spirit. So, different
words are used to explain. Excellence is an expression of
man's natural search. Non attachment makes it fruitful.

Is this why different religions state the same Truth in different ways

Yes.

Now, how will these ideas help market a product?

The product is a means of satisfying a customer's need. The need and not sales of product is the focus for the customer. Both research for new ways of satisfying need and product delivery should focus on this. This will lead to closeness or oneness with customer and give delight.

How is this different from traditional theory?

There is nothing new about *Purusharthas*, too. The first *Purushartha* of righteous conduct makes them useful for society. They result in selfish interest being fulfilled so as to fulfill society's interest and highest interest too. They emerge from pure intentions, awareness of society.

Are *Purusharthas* not too restrictive for humans?

In fact they impart freedom. Instead of setting rules of conduct for each specific task, they enable Truth about righteous conduct to emerge from within man. As nature of things is to change, such ability allows for change in expression of strategy in work and life, core being same.

Your book explains many things about ancient Indian tradition. Many object to its image worship. How can such a tradition be profitable for society?
Image worship is based on the experience of seeing the macrocosm within the microcosm without using imagination to visualise excellence. Thus, images serve the same purpose as metaphors or similes in language.
They illustrate, amplify and clarify. Joy is in the relationship with the image, not in the image. Just as not just any child but her own child makes a mother happy. The idea is to expand this feeling towards everything.

Are there any examples of behavior that this book recommends in companies, or is this a theory?
Many people and businesses, too, may be following such ideas. A formal theory can help make them as examples. Academicians give examples which may integrate partly.

Can you give examples? This is only a generalisation
Rosabeth Kanter of Harvard gives examples. Raj Sisodia and Whole Foods CEO seek to raise consciousness. McGrath talks of Milliken. A theory formalises a direction for study.

But, don't their examples show that some business people are self actualised?
Of course they are on the path. Their personal satisfaction and joy is evidence of this. Self actualisation is as much a journey as a destination. It is a continuous process to be relived.

**Can we conclude that such companies
will not be impacted by recession?**
A few practices by a few people do not give
a complete idea about a company. Recession
is the impact of collective consciousness. The
totality of intentions and activities is needed.

**How do we understand this totality –
which prevents recession?**
This book seeks to start the search for such a totality.
This is a continuous search. The ideas to begin the
search must be correct. This book gives such ideas.

What new focus changes ideas that lead to recession?
The difference is in training the mind and developing
perception of the imperceptible impact on society of
actions. This is imparting the ability to 'C' correctly.

5

HOW IS EXCELLENCE OUR LATENT TALENT?

Ancient wisdom:
That excellence that you think is outside is within you.
Chapter 6 gives details.

Management Ideas:
The authors of the book 'In Search of Excellence'
(R.H. Waterman Jr. and T. Peters) created a 7S model
used by consultancy firm McKinsey. The core of this
model is 'Shared Values' which guides business (firms)
to achieve the best. This search of excellence brings
out innate goodness in man when he is at work.

Good Thoughts 🎵 *are music for the Soul*

Good words 🎵 *are music for others/ listeners*

Good deeds 🎵 *are music for society*

The Unity of Good Thoughts, Good Words, Good Deeds is the Strategy for living life – which when applied at work prevents all problems in society – including recession. Their implementation transforms human behavior to follow the dictum of ancient wisdom:

HELP EVER, HURT NEVER

If this rule of Chapter 6 is followed in each action, the contents of Chapters 1 to 5 have been absorbed.

What is the main task the book is designed for?
It is to bring together ideas that can unfold
the excellence hidden in man.

Ancient ideas are no longer relevant why use them?
Can speaking the truth or following morality be
considered not relevant? If this is the conviction, then
there is no way to stop crime, recession, social conflict
etc. Giving primacy to these ideas in education is the
concept of ancient wisdom which is being used here.

How do ancient ideas become relevant today?
Their daily practice and use will make them
relevant. The fabric of society is woven with the
thread of Truth and Morality. If this thread is
broken, society will wear tattered clothes.

How do ancient ideas promote excellence today?
Ancient wisdom promotes sincerity of purpose to
augment use of skills. This sincerity includes studying
the impact of actions undertaken on society. Excellence
results when individual skills promote society's welfare.

Does only ancient wisdom bring out excellence in us?
Any set of actions that ensure prosperity that does
not harm society or nature brings out excellence
hidden in man. Keeping the environmental
degradation and social problems in mind, we are
just seeking to revive the ideas which many feel
strongly about. Many do act on these ideas without
being exposed formally to ancient wisdom.

Are you saying that these ideas are within us?
When speaking the truth or acting morally gives
us inner peace and satisfaction, what does it
prove? These ideas are already within each of us.
Wisdom taught us to keep reinforcing them in daily
behavior - in fact in each and every action. This brings
out the best within man to benefit him and others.

So, excellence is inside for education to bring it out?
Just like seed sprouts and germinates to grow into a
tree which bears flowers and fruit, this process, too,
takes time and effort. It is a process and not an event.

If marketing or strategy theory is same what is new?
The practice of theory should be with excellence. When
intention is pure – selfishness withers excellence results.

**Can you describe how in a particular situation
seeing 'Cing'what data will bring out excellence?**
First, for any field there must be a steady application of the
mind to train it in skills needed for that task, profession
or discipline. This is given by secular education today.
With this skill there must be sincerity in the search for
excellence – without the veil of selfishness. Then, many
Truths emerge from within. There is always a sea of data or
information or choices available, but to the sincere aspirant
of excellence only that data or choice or information will
appeal which can add value to society. When the inner
instinct is to Help Ever, Hurt Never the choices are made
within the mind. Those actions emerge that add value in a
meaningful manner. Sincerity is necessary to keep working
towards perfection in all that one seeks and does. This is a
process that is continuous within man and in his search.

How will both society and I recognise excellence?
The feeling of satisfaction that comes by self sacrifice or
the sacrifice of selfishness gives immense satisfaction.
Society may recognise it slowly but man recognises
it immediately. This feeling satiates the soul. Selfish
satisfaction is insatiable. Both are habit forming.

**So, success can come through any means
but excellence emerges from Truth?**
Yes. This is the Truth about man and this is within
man. This truth is that he gets satisfaction from
following moral behavior. Of course, many get
temporary satisfaction by stealing or cheating. It may
give money and status. There are many examples of
people with money who are not satisfied. So, the link
between wealth and satisfaction is not clear. However,
if wealth is earned through righteous conduct it gives
satisfaction to man and creates satisfaction in society.

**Can you give a simple guide of action that creates
such satisfaction in man and balance in society?**
The ancient wisdom of *Bhagavad Geeta* states:
"Karmanye vadhikaraste ma phaleshu kadachana".
The simple rule of performing actions without
an eye on reward is the key. An action should be
performed because it is the right thing to do at that
time. Desire for success should be guided by non
attachment to fruit of actions. Then, because only
the right thing that needs to be done will be done –
success if it comes will become excellence.

6

WHAT DO WE HAVE TO SEE ABOUT A BUSINESS?

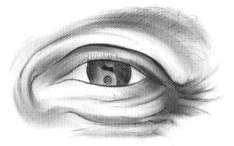

How does the eye of modern management see life and work through the lens of ancient wisdom?

Ancient Wisdom:
Many verses in Bhagavad Geeta *impart the ability to see reality of the Self. They freely use the words* pashyati, pashyami and 'yah pashyati sah pashyati'– *all of which deal with imparting the ability to 'C' or see.*

New management idea:
Management: Man + Age + Me(a)nt. Man in this age is meant to actualize or realise his potential for excellence.

Ancient Wisdom sees the world through the principles of Yin and Yang, too. They are opposite yet complimentary.

Examples are day and night, cycle of seasons (cold/hot).

In ancient Indian tradition there is Prakriti *and* Purusha. *The former is ever changing, the latter never changing.*

1st C: The never changing aspect of society is the need for co-operation (even among opposites).

2nd C: The never changing aspect in ever changing society is a focus on excellence with concern for society.

3rd C: When human response or competitive response is guided by the need for compatibility it creates balance.

4th C: The compatibility of day and night, cycles of seasons creates balance in nature. Similarly the compatibility of different inner nature of men and their different skill sets create balance if they lead to a response that is focused on excellence with a concern for society. This leads to the best within man emerging enabling him to realise his potential of excellence. Thus man and society achieve balance simultaneously.

Only if the focus of education is on each individual's transformation can society be transformed.

What is there to 'see' in a business? Either you do business or you do not...What is to be seen?
A business is not a machine. It is run by humans with an attitude. This attitude should be of serving society. Does everybody see this? Individuality and humility coexist to serve our need of interdependence. This is to be seen.

Can we get a more practical answer?
When a customer enters a shop do you see profit walking in or an opportunity to serve? How to see a customer's needs and motivation? Different perceptions lead to different products. Values give unity in diversity.

Can we get a philosophical basis of such an answer?
In an address to Soto priests in Japan Holiness Dalai Lama described five paths given by Buddha in the Heart Sutra. The third path is 'The Path of seeing'.

Usually, such words hide multiple dimensions – can you give another explanation?
The ancient Indian philosophies were referred to as *Darshan*. For example the six philosophies are called *Shad Darshan*. The word *Darshan* means sight, ability to 'C'!

**Is there no expression in English that warns
us not to believe the visible truth fully?**
"None as blind as those who have eyes" – So,
'C' carefully! The body follows the dictates of
the mind. Is the mind visible? Though unseen,
can anybody doubt its existence? So, the unseen
phenomenon is existent and maybe a more important
determinant than that which is seen. Also, do you
see an opportunity where others see a threat? Can
you visualise some goodness within the bad?

**What are the paths, including 'C'ing,
given by Buddha in Heart Sutra?**
According to speeches of His Holiness The Dalai
Lama, these are: the path of accumulation, the
path of preparation, the path of seeing, the path
of meditation and the path of no more learning.
The path of seeing correctly opens higher ones.

Do you see anything wrong with earning wealth?
There is nothing wrong with earning wealth. If
it emerges from serving society selflessly, with
excellence, it leads to the higher goal. Process
of earning wealth can sensitise man to serve
society selflessly. Earning wealth should be the
byproduct of action, not the primary cause.

So, earning wealth sensitises – but, towards what?
Can wealth give happiness? Can it remove misery?
Some wealth is important. So, *Artha* is a goal
of life. The inability of wealth to impart true
happiness prepares man for higher search. The
process of earning wealth is the first step. If the
first step is in the wrong direction, the destination
will not be reached. So, work selflessly.

**Can you share views of any thinker – other than
ancient Indian or ancient Greek – about this?**
Khalil Gibran from Lebanon writes something
similar: "... Is not dread of thirst when your well
is full the thirst that is unquenchable?..." Worldly
wealth does not quench the thirst if greed guides.

**The book states: 'C' unity is the final experience.
It starts with a study of man. Where is the unity
in a study of man and study of the firm?**
Diagram 4.0 demonstrates this commonality
through a Trinity of Five. Five life breaths, life
forces and five things common to the human body
and the body of the firm are given. The different
dimensions of each (as applicable to man and
firm separately) are shown. When both man and
firm are studied and understood in a common
framework of ideas the unity becomes obvious.

How does man 'C' correctly?

The easiest way to see correctly is to 'do' correctly and 'be' correct at all times. This is righteous conduct or *Dharma.* Thus the ancient Indian wisdom: Do good, be good, see good. Kabir, an ancient Indian wise man has said that when he set out to find bad in the world he was unable to see it outside. When he peeped inside his heart he discovered that all that was bad was inside him. Thus the invisible mind is the source of bad thoughts. Controlling bad thoughts is in the power of man. He is responsible for his thoughts and must control them. Only then society can benefit. However he should not have *Karma Adwaitha.* He must use discrimination in world.

Why is the book giving spiritual knowledge?

The dictionary defines 'spirit' as that which gives life to vital organs. Similarly, spirit behind an act gives meaning and direction to action. This spirit is not found in textbooks but within man himself. Why should speaking Truth or acting on its dictates be considered a spiritual practice? It is a normal practice, but it deals with the spirit of man's intentions and observations. Hence, it becomes spiritual, too – as it gives meaning and direction to man's actions in society.

After seeing a unity between study of man and the firm where he works what are the next steps?

First there must be unity in thought, word and deed of man. Then there should be unity with customer, co-workers, suppliers etc. This comes through co-operation (which is the first thing to see). This unity that emerges through co-operation must be given a focus of serving the customer's needs in a unique way. This focus should be guided by a concern for society. This is the second thing to see. This leads to the third thing to see the competitive response. The ideal of this is that the response should be so elevated that there should be no competition possible to such unique excellence. Only the past work should be the competition. Then the final thing to see is the compatibility of this response to the needs of society and environment. This is like expanding the human heart to fill it with larger concerns of others merged with a larger concern for excellence. Diagrams of chapter 5 demonstrate how this happens.

Can education afford to be values neutral?

If for life in society values are not needed, education can be values neutral. However, this will lead to destruction of society sooner or later. So values are valuable for all.

The book states that there should be no dogmatic approach. Is 4C approach not another dogma?

All endeavours of man should be based on truth and morality. The 4C approach is based on this idea. Diagram 0.30 shows how it emerges from Truth and leads to balance within man and in society. Chapter 6 shows that it is not a dogmatic approach. Even if we begin with simple things to remember about man and society as given in the first few sections of Chapter 6, we will come to conclusions similar to the 4C Approach. It is thus a convenient approach to use – not a dogma. Different ways of understanding merge in this approach. This has been shown and the validity of using a fourfold approach has also been tested by a study of the most important scriptures of this tradition. Diagram 6.6 shows how the call of action of all scripture leads to the two criteria for judging human actions (given in Exhibit 4 at the beginning of Chapter 7 – as validity of *Moksha* or self actualisation in action). This convergence of ideas is the task of Chapter 6. Such a convergence with science, spirituality, and the real world is dealt in Chapter 7.

After 1+5≥6 (156) questions, now a summary:

A clenched fists power is more than sum of five fingers'
Add to it the power of an arm...this one arm and five
fingers (in a fist) can now use the power of the body
to give a punch to remove ignorance of the mind.

7

WHAT DOES THE SUMMARY
SUMMARISE?

Ancient wisdom:
"Do aur do ka jod hameshan chaar kahan hota hai
Soojh boojh walon ko thodi naadani de Maula"

*Ancient Sufi style lyric: The summation $\sum$ of
two and two is not always four. O Lord! Give
the knowledgeable some innocence too.*

Management idea:
*In management psychology when the whole maybe
greater than ($\geq$) the sum of parts it is called GESTALT.*

Ancient Wisdom and Management idea:
The Gestalt, if all try, prevents recession, other problems

1. *When the sum of actions of many individuals working in society (depicted by symbol $\sum$) reflects a spirit of co-operation this is the first C of management.*

2. *When such groups of individuals in a company or firm work with a focus on excellence with a concern for society, this is the second C of management.*

3. *The output of such groups or individuals, as a result of the above two processes is called a response or competitive response. This is the third C of management.*

4. *When this competitive response is compatible with the needs of society and nature the 4th C of management ensures a Gestalt that can surprise all...*

4Cs emerge from four goals of life. Ancient wisdom guides mans actions towards fulfilling them. They lead to balance within man and in society. Every person has different skills at work and different requirements as a customer. The perfect matching of skills and requirements (through cooperation and focus concern) leads to harmony, balance in society as man becomes wise. Then, total sum of actions ($\sum$) is more than ($\geq$) sum of individual actions. Unlike this process of addition of skills and talents to benefit all, crime, recession etc subtract from others welfare to benefit only a few. Such behavior harms society and may harm perpetrators, too.

Why is the summary given here and not in the book?
There is a separate feeling when you look at something
from near and from far. Both should be enjoyable.
Reading the book is looking from near. Having a
summary separately allows enjoying the book from
a distance. From the summary you can go back to
the book to understand the same thing in a different
perspective or understand it better this time.

**Why are some questions about the book
answered here and not in the book?**
While reading the book the logic of the book
is followed. However, some questions should
keep forming at the back of the mind. The book
is not the best place to answer them – as it has
its own flow. But these questions are important
and need an answer. Their answers, here, allow
an enjoyment of the book – from a distance.

The importance of ancient wisdom: Case study of 2008

Ancient wisdom postulates that fortunes of man and society are interlinked. If education does not instill this belief in its curriculum, both suffer. Let us take the example of 2008 recession:

Many perpetrators of events that led to it were highly qualified and skilled graduates and post graduates from well known educational institutions. Their decisions led to the 2008 recession. What is sad for them is not the misery and unemployment that was created (for many would say – 'I don't give a damn!) but the fact that many of them became unemployed too. Even more grievous for them was that some of them will become unemployable, too! If this inevitable fact they could 'C' while they were taking actions prior to the recession – would their choices still be the same?

If their education had inculcated this vision or sight as a part of strategy of living life and working, maybe things would be different. The summary here is designed to inculcate such a conviction among students – to prepare them for both life and work. Then, they cannot harm themselves and others. The benefit of hindsight of events that followed the recession is the best reaffirmation that ancient wisdom has solutions like the 4C Approach.

SUMMARY

The Summary of this book is in three parts:

a) **Why is the book written?**
b) **What does the book say?**
c) **How do its conclusions apply to life?**

(a) Why is the book written?

The book gives an idea of how to transform man's experience of life. It gives concrete answers to a few questions: "Why does crisis impact a society repeatedly?" "Why do steps taken to stem a crisis not succeed fully?" "Have we learnt enough lessons from last financial crisis or is a second one in the making?" "Can we design a study which prevents crisis in society?"

It seeks to prepare man and mankind for any crisis that a society is likely to face. This is done by restoring in education the capacity to transform man.

The question it seeks to ask is:

- The global economic crisis occurred despite Management professionals with degrees from top business schools taking decisions.
- Similarly, many global problems like environmental degradation, social conflicts etc. occur despite educated performing key roles.

- Keeping this in view, who takes responsibility for a crisis in society? Regulators and laws follow events to prevent future ones. But future events again need new laws. So, laws keep chasing violations. What can make self correction occur *within* managers and firms? Which way of thinking can give *discrimination* and guide man towards action that **prevents** a crisis?

Who will design this way of thinking? Where to draw inspiration for it?

- Can we start with education saying: "the buck stops here"?

If society does not ask difficult questions or accept responsibility for a crisis, can any civilisation survive for long? Society, usually, entrusts education with the task of transforming man.

Therefore:

- To seek answers, can we learn from a civilisation that has survived?

The author chooses the ancient Indian civilisation. Some management ideas of the '90's are shared. For, top decision makers were armed for recession by business schools with such ideas. These integrate with ancient Indian ones – here.

The reasons of choosing ancient Indian tradition are given in Section (a) of Background – in Introduction of book. It shares basic ideas which enable a civilisation to survive. Their implications on education are useful and are, therefore, given in detail.

The terms used in this tradition are introduced or refreshed in this chapter. The book interprets them in a contemporary setting with familiar words.

Later chapters of the book use ideas explained in this Background section. Chapters 1 to 5 also incorporate them. They enable Man to manage life, firms to manage business and society to manage balance with nature. All at the same time! Such balance – within man, society and nature – is a non zero sum game. Profit of one does not become loss of the other. This idea is central to both education and living life. It is shown, through diagrams, in Chapter 5 – leading to Diagram 5.9. This shows simultaneous balance in man and society.

Education helps discover Individuality through the path of humility. The ego of having exclusive knowledge, without character, can lead to misuse for personal gains. This is harmful for balance in society. Collectively, if Individuality finds expression in a context of benefitting the nation (nationality), it leads to balance. One expression of nationality is national competitive advantage – which Michael Porter studies. Its idea if used with Truth, Morality and caring for all can lead to simultaneous balance within man and in society.

As everybody contributes to balance in society, target audience of this book is everybody.

- Therefore, everybody should read this book. Just as business is a small part of life, two third of the book is about life. Only a third is about hard core ideas of management. It shows how business emerges from life and merges back in it. This brings balance within man and society.

(b) What does the book say?

The book is about **two ideas**:

- * Part A: It details, in Chapter 1, how **values merge into strategy** (of both – life and business) and
- * Part B: It explains (in Chapter 2, 3, 4 and 5) **how strategy emerges from values.**

<u>The book's Structure is:</u> The Introduction asks the right questions about Education. Background within Introduction explains the purpose of this study.

The book emerges from an understanding of ancient Indian tradition. Chapter 6 shows how management ideas merge into it once again. Just like a wave from the ocean. The synopsis and Introduction (and Chapters 6 and 7) are twice the size of the management approach the book proposes. This represents that 4C Approach has to apply to – and merge in – life of man.

The book itself is in two parts. Chapter 1 belongs to Part A. The 4C Approach, elaborated in Chapters 2 to 5, belong to Part B.

The 4C Approach based on 4 *Purusharthas* or goals of life: A (re)new(ed!) management approach

Chapters 2 to 5 translate idea of four *Purusharthas* into words and ideas used by modern management. This helps integration of ancient Indian thought with theory. These *Purusharthas* of *Dharma, Artha, Kama* and *Moksha* work best in pairs. *Dharma* with *Artha* is one pair while *Kama* with *Moksha* is the second. Righteous conduct guides economic activity while desire fulfilment is guided by Self actualisation. Crisis in society occurs with wrong pairing of *Artha* with *Kama*. Then, economic activity is guided by unrestrained desires only – without righteous conduct.

The **First *Purushartha*** of *Dharma* has many dimensions – righteous conduct is one of them. Co-operation represents *Dharma.* This begins integration with current management theory.

Thus, Co-operation is across three fields:

- Within man's mind – as co-operation between thought, word and deed.

- Within man's body – as co-operation among all body parts enabling action.
- Within the body of society (again in two dimensions) – First dimension is co-operation by all constituents of society. The second dimension is more important. That is co-operating in the right spirit as represented by unity or co-operation of thought word and deed. Co-operation creates balance within the firm, society and between nations. The spirit of unity is more important than an outward show of unity. Co-operation begins within man, advances to co-operation between men (in firm and society) and towards co-operation between nations. Finally, man must learn to co-operate with nature to prevent environmental degradation. This will create balance within man, between men i.e. in society, between nations and balance between man and nature. In this manner a civilisation can survive. The ancient Indian tradition helps man achieve this balance through education. Therefore, we choose it as the source of this study.

Porter describes benefits of co-operation in achieving the task of creating competitive advantage for a nation. This expands the concept from within man to the firm, society and nation.

Another way of looking at *Dharma* is as follows. *Dharma* promotes balance. If man follows it, there is balance within man. If society follows it, society is in balance. Co-operation is the basis of balance in society and can, therefore, be the aspect of *Dharma* to begin our study. Thus, it is the 1st C of management.

Chapter 6.4(a) describes how ancient Indian texts understand co-operation. *Yoga* means coming together of which co-operation is the basis – even in thought, word and deed! The path of *Yoga* is described differently in different texts according to context. However, those who can create the union (of 'Self' with its Source – emanating from co-operation of Self with teachings of the Source) are *Yogis*. When *Yoga* (which also means spiritual path) is basis of learning, one's excellence is furthered by adding to it excellence in others. This togetherness or union can make individuals and society experience co-operation. It leads to compatibility. This inner meaning of *Yoga* is also a guide for choosing co-operation as *Dharma*. No wonder *Bhagavad Gita* refers to its chapters as *Yoga*.

The inner meaning of the **Second *Purushartha*** of *Artha* in this tradition is not just economic activity. It is man's declaration of distinction from others! This is focus of the word *Artha*. When pure selfishness is not the prime reason for action and man has a larger concern, he declares distinction from animal kingdom. Therefore focussed Concern is taken to imply *Artha*. It includes a focus on the customer and a concern for his needs. Also, a focus on quality with a concern for quality of life. Then, products do not harm the customer, community, or environment in the long run. A focus on creating value with a concern for environment of man, customer and society ensures this.

Diagrams 3.2, 3.2, 3.4, 4.7 and 4.8 depict the focus on the customer in this approach.

A focus on Self Preservation with a concern for Self Satisfaction may be basis of action – for man and firm. Self Satisfaction is the experience of adding value in a unique way, with excellence, through selfless action. Scientists, innovators and those adding value continuously – to themselves and society – can be driven by this experience. Greed or selfishness, then, may not motivate them. Such a focussed Concern has to permeate the 'five life breaths of business'. It leads to constant re-engineering in a dynamic environment when customer has new and emerging needs. Diagram 3.1 depicts it while Diagram 3.5 depicts the process of focussed Concern.

Self Satisfaction gives meaning to work and life. Quality gives meaning to Production. Business process Re-engineering gives meaning to sub-optimal processes etc. What gives meaning to business? A focus on and a concern for quality, customer, purpose of business (Self preservation to self satisfaction and serving society through customers) gives it. What gives meaning to purpose of life? Self Satisfaction by doing yeoman service to society gives it. When selfless action, through excellence gives man's declaration of distinction, meaning of life is realised. Thus, focussed Concern is the 2nd C of management. It is not for firm, alone – but also for man.

The Fourth *Purushartha* of *Moksha* is the guide for the **Third *Purushartha*** of *Kama* or desire fulfilment. The two parts of word *Moksha* reveal its meaning. It is done by elimination of attachment (*Moha* is attachment and *Kshaya* implies its end). Excellence in performing a task is for the inner joy or Self Satisfaction that leads to Self Realisation or *Moksha*. The result of any action is an uncontrollable variable. Concentration by doing duty in the best possible manner is the ideal. The result, then, is not so important. This is the inner meaning of the pairing of *Kama* and *Moksha*. It is also the teaching of *Bhagavad Gita*. Excellence, therefore, is to be achieved for its own sake. It should not be guided by greed – thus removing the cause of financial crisis which had greed as its basis. Diagram 4.9 compares the different understanding of Excellence in the 3C Approach. 3C Approach is bereft of a concept of Self Actualisation, non- attachment or *Moksha* unlike the 4C Approach.

Kama or desire fulfilment in the corporate world results in a firm's Competitive Response. This is 3rd C of management. The 4C Approach shifts how man understands competition. It believes that competitor only gives the first benchmark. This benchmark unfolds man and firms Individuality in a direction. This broad vision emerges when man, guided by values, indulges in Porter's Optimisation effort as part of strategy. This overarches mindless maximisation of profit to Optimisation. This shows in product design and production, optimal use of resources, optimal profit etc.

Fig 0.11 onwards till Fig 0.16 details an understanding of the nature of creation in the ancient Indian tradition. The nature of creation is ever changing. It's ever changing nature has an influence on man's socialisation. It also influences his inner drive, growth of Knowledge and information available. More knowledge influences technology development. The ability to develop products increases. Diagram 3.2 shows it as the interplay between influencers and the customer. When education is taking customers upwards (in Maslow's hierarchy of needs) – it is the basis of a Creative Market.

Education trains man's intellect to increase the capacity of discrimination to transform the heart of man (shown in Fig 0.5, Fig 0.9). This Discrimination is individual discrimination and at societal and universal level. Practice of Truth, Conduct, Peace and Love, thus, must not be selfish. This makes man's rise in Maslow's hierarchy of human needs. Here, humility leads man to discover his Individuality. The ever changing nature of creation has an impact on customer. It influences 'emerging needs' as well as 'current needs'. Diagrams 3.3 and 3.4 (in the Chapter of focussed Concern) and Diagrams 4.7 and 4.8 (in Chapter of Competitive Response or 3rd C) show this. The seat of desire is in the heart of man. The intellect seeks ways to fulfill them. Education's purpose is to transform the heart. So, heart is the market. To transform society, desires should be transformed. This is the Mark or target that marketing seeks to Get. Marketing, thus, is a difficult subject involving all human desires and their transformation by products and services that are uplifting.

Understanding the fourth *Purushartha* of *Moksha* is not possible if the above conclusions do not apply to life. Competitive Response (Points 1 to 3 above) is the application of Strategy and marketing. How does Self Actualisation, given in Point 4 apply to life – especially in Marketing?

(c) How do the conclusions apply to life?

We know that Strategy applies to life when there is unity of thought, word and deed. How does its use in marketing apply to life – helping man transform?

Mere hearing a lecture on marketing (without reflecting or responding) is passive, not active learning. Such passive participation is *'tamasic'* or associated with dull brains. The individual's effort to turn the thought over in his mind, trying to assimilate it makes a person active or *'rajasic'*. When man achieves the experience of purity of intention this is *'sathwic'*. Therefore, marketing is at three levels depending on the qualities of the student. Its use is also at three levels. Dull students gain knowledge by analysing the objective world alone. Active knowledge serves the best interests of society. Finally, purifying intent and urge of man is the goal. Action that arises from such purified intentions leads to highest wisdom.

Chapter 6.4(c) lists these 3 stages of competitive response that lead to compatibility. This is the true understanding of competitive response. Absorbing the idea can occur in 3 different ways depending on qualities of the seeker.

Strategy integrates with 4C approach here. Marketing ideas, taught till early '90s, are recalled. However, they are not commented upon.

Finally, the only competition is with one self. The desire for self improvement is the correct understanding of competitive response. This will result in continuously improving unique products. They will be focussed on either serving the same need or new/emerging needs of the customer. However, they will do it in newer and better ways. Thus, they will satisfy the Individuality of the customer, the firm and individuals in the firm.

The **Fourth Purushartha** of *Moksha*, like the First *Purushartha* i.e. *Dharma*, creates balance. Therefore, both pair with a *Purushartha* that guides man's daily actions. While *Dharma* promotes balance by guiding man towards the true meaning of his action, *Moksha* is balance itself! While *Dharma* concentrates on fulfilment of duty, *Moksha* refers to non – attachment to result of action. Both of them, as guides, make man's actions compatible with needs of society and create a balance with nature. When men and firms act on first 3C's in desired manner, society benefits from Advantage of Compatibility: the 4thC of management. It is shown in Diagram 5.9 of Chapter 5. All diagrams (starting with man as a customer – rising in Maslow's need Hierarchy), from Diagram 5.2 onwards, build up to Diagram 5.9.

The ancient texts of Upanishads refer to converging self interest with a higher interest as well as highest enlightened interest of society. This is called converging *Swartha* with *Parartha* and *Parmartha*. Chapter 6 discusses it. It is the law of seed and tree. Expansion is the nature of creation (shown in Fig 0.13). The highest desire of expansion of the tree is fulfilled as a seed. And, the highest desire of expansion of the seed finds fulfilment when it becomes a tree. The convergence of self interest with highest interest of society makes all participants enjoy benefits of Compatibility Advantage. It is expressed through this law of nature. At this destination all paths of excellence of ancient Indian tradition i.e. *Karma, Bhakti* and *Jnana* merge. Chapter6 explains it.

Conclusion of the book:

Chapter 6 gives the Conclusion or the Highest Truth towards which education guides man. The highest truth of unity of creation is not easily understood or experienced. So, intermediate stages are important. The most important transformation is of man's desires.

The ancient Indian tradition tackles wish fulfilment (the basis of the 3rd C or competitive response) in the *Yajur Veda*'s Sri *Rudram*. Here, recitation of *Chamakam* (which deals with fulfilment of all noble wishes) follows the recitation of *Namakam*. In the latter, man does *namah* – or bows to all in creation. When bowing to all is the basis of desire fulfilment, a cleansing process occurs within man. Impact of action on others guides man's desires. Even before desires are formed. Desire creation, then, cannot harm others. Of course, the *Vedic* sacrifices (interpreted as inner sacrifice by man – of his ignorance, bad thoughts and qualities) go with recitation of this holy text. They prepare man for the experience of unity of creation. The advanced ancient Indian texts of *Upanishads* and *Atma Vidya* catalyse this experience.

Knowledge is like an ocean. Each discipline is like a wave. This chapter shows how the wave of management merges back in ancient Indian tradition. Chapter 6 merges these ideas back into an understanding of life.

The ability to experience Truth is the purpose of education. The path of experiencing Dualism begins a journey towards non-dualistic nature of world. In this path man understands that if he harms the world he is harming himself only. Diagram 6.11 shows the plan of this book with 4C's of Management and life. It also details, simply, what these 4Cs imply as guides for action.

Chapter 6 also addresses those who are likely to say: "This book does not make sense" by devoting a section to them. Diagram 6.12 shows how man, enriched with experience, spreads it through education. Education relates to what is within man i.e. Body, mind Soul. Also, it relates to what is within the world which can be tackled using the four *Purusharthas*. In this manner, the flow of education integrates with flow of life.

The importance of human body and lessons for using it are given in this Chapter. Important things to remember about man and society are also shared. The ancient Indian tradition gives three paths to achieving goal of life. They are *Karma*, *Bhakti* and *Jnana* – Activity, devotion and Knowledge/ wisdom seeking. The Chapter shows how they merge in the business of living.

The core of all processes of the firm and society is Shared Values. The core of shared values is Selfless Love. Fig 0.29 in Background shows how it emerges.

The book's basis:

The spirit (or intent) behind man's action is often not visible and benefits or harms society. Cleansing the spirit or intent of man is the spiritual task of this tradition. Therefore its epics and text's interpretation given here enables this book to be a common source of study for all: spiritual aspirants, students of philosophy, social work, education and management, among other disciplines.

This merger of Knowledge with practical aspect of how to live life is the essence of education. This book tries to capture it. Of course, the most important lessons can never taught by a book. Chapter 7 begins with this recognition. The Realisation that man gets about his potential is the result of Awareness or total understanding that emerges through transformation. How is this transformation achieved in the ancient Indian tradition? It does not come through study alone – it comes mainly through practice! Some practices of this tradition that result in this transformation are given. For those who seek to use this book. These transform the spirit and are spiritual practices.

The book chooses a single Source of study – both in modern management thought as well as ancient Indian tradition.

The use of a single Source gives benefit of usage of common terminology, ideas, concepts and understanding across a wide range of topics. This prevents confusion or misinterpretation and leads to ease of research.

<u>Testing Truth of ideas – when theory becomes practice</u>

These ancient Indian ideas of management and life have been put to practice through some projects by the Source of this study. They have put the principle of 'unity in thought, word and deed' into practice and give force to this Paper's conclusions.

Printed in the United States
By Bookmasters